The Potential Principle

SCRIPTURE REFERENCE GUIDE

Edwin Louis Cole

A Division of Harrison House, Inc.
Tulsa, Oklahoma

The Potential Principle Scripture Reference Guide
ISBN 0-89274-365-4

Edwin Louis Cole Ministries

International Headquarters
P. O. Box 825
Corona del Mar, CA 92625

Southwest Offices
P. O. Box 610588
Dallas, TX 75261

Published by HONOR BOOKS
A Division of Harrison House, Inc.
P. O. Box 35035
Tulsa, Oklahoma 74153

Printed in the United States of America.

CONTENTS

THE POTENTIAL PRINCIPLE

Outline and Reference Guide

Chapter 1 - DREAM THE IMPOSSIBLE DREAM

A. God does everything according to a pattern, based on a principle.

Example: **Heb. 8:5**

Who serve unto the example and shadow of heavenly things, as Moses was admonished of God when he was about to make the tabernacle: for, See, saith he, that thou make all things according to the pattern showed to thee in the mount.

Gal. 6:16 (Living)

May God's mercy and peace be upon all of you who live by this principle and upon those everywhere who are really God's own.

Also **I Chron. 28:11; Exod 25:8,9**

1. All principles of human society are basically Kingdom Principles.

Col. 1:16,17

For by him were all things created, that are in heaven, and that are in earth, visible and invisible . . . all things were created by him, and for him:

Also **I Cor. 8:6, Rom. 11:36**

2. The more we base our lives on principles the straighter our course will be.

Prov. 4:11,12

I have taught thee in the way of wisdom; I have led thee in right paths. When thou goest, thy steps shall not be hindered; and when thou runnest thou shalt not stumble.

3. Truth and reality are synonymous.

B. God uses dreams.

Joel 2:28

. . . and your sons and your daughters shall prophesy, your old men shall dream dreams, your young men shall see visions.

1. Men who dream become builders.

Example - **Neh. 2:5**

And I said unto the king, If it please the king, and if thy servant have found favor in thy sight, that thou wouldest send me unto Judah, unto the city of my fathers' sepulchers, that I may build it.

a. Despite ridicule and persecution they continue on.

Example: **Neh. 2:19-20**

But when Sanballat the Horonite, and Tobiah the servant, the Ammonite, and Geshem the Arabian, heard it, they laughed us to scorn and despised us . . .
Then answered I them, The God of heaven, he will prosper us; therefore we his servants will arise and build: but ye have no portion, nor right nor memorial, in Jerusalem.

Example: **Neh. 6:2,3**

. . . Sanballat and Geshem . . . thought to do me mischief. And I sent messengers unto them, saying, I am doing a great work, so that I cannot come down: why should the work cease, whilst I leave it, and come down to you?

b. They translate their dreams into reality.

Neh. 6:15

So the wall was finished in the twenty and fifth day of the month Elul, in fifty and two days.

2. God gave Joseph a dream.

Gen. 37:5,9

And Joseph dreamed a dream, and he told it his brethren: and they hated him yet the more . . .
And he dreamed yet another dream, and told it his brethren . . .

Chapter 1 (cont.)

3. His dream created an image in his mind which ultimately became a reality.

Gen. 37:7

For, behold, we were binding sheaves in the field, and lo, my sheaf arose, and also stood upright; and, behold, your sheaves stood round about, and made obeisance to my sheaf.

Gen. 43:26

And when Joseph came home, they (his brothers) . . . bowed themselves to him to the earth.

4. In the same way God wants to develop the potential of your life.

Eph. 2:10

For we are his workmanship, created in Christ Jesus unto good works, which God has before ordained that we should walk in them.

Phil. 3:12

Not as though I had already attained, either were already perfect: but I follow after, if that I may apprehend that for which also I am apprehended of Christ Jesus.

Also **Phil. 2:12,13**

C. Dreams are important.

1. One of the ways God speaks to us.

Num. 12:6

And he said, Hear now my words: If there be a prophet among you, I the Lord will make myself known unto him in a vision, and will speak unto him in a dream.

2. God promises to give us the desires of our hearts.

Prov. 10:24

. . . the desire of the righteous shall be granted.

Ps. 145:19

He will fulfill the desire of them that fear him: . . .

Also **Ps. 21:2**

a. He authors those desires.

Ps. 37:4

Delight thyself also in the Lord; and he shall give thee the desires of thine heart.

b. He implements those desires as we submit to His Lordship.

Ps. 37:5

Commit thy way unto the Lord; trust also in him; and he shall bring it to pass.

3. Dreams motivate change.

a. Dreams are part of the very nature of man's spirit.

Prov. 29:18

Where there is no vision, the people perish . . .

b. A shattered dream is devastating to an individual.

Prov. 13:12

Hope deferred maketh the heart sick, but when the desire cometh, it is a tree of life.

4. Dreams that are nothing more than fantasies cannot stand the test of reality.

Eccl. 5:7 (N.A.S.B.)

For in the multitude of dreams and many words there are also divers vanities; but fear thou God.

D. Dreams and leadership.

1. Joseph's dream was a revelation of leadership.

See **Gen. 37:7,9**

2. God prepares leaders through testing.

Heb. 2:10

For it became him, for whom are all things, and by whom are all things, in bringing many sons unto glory, to make the captain of their salvation perfect through sufferings.

a. There is a price to pay in leadership.

Phil. 2:5-8

Let this mind be in you, which was also in Christ Jesus: who, being in the form of God, thought it not robbery to be equal with God: But made himself of no reputation, and took upon him the form of a servant, and was made in the likeness of men: And being found in the fashion as a man, he humbled himself, and became obedient unto death, even the death of the cross.

b. Ruling the spirit is a requirement of successful leadership.

Prov. 16:32

He that is slow to anger is better than the mighty; and he that ruleth his spirit than he that taketh a city.

Prov. 25:28

He that hath no rule over his own spirit is like a city that is broken down, and without walls.

Also **Prov. 19:11; Eccl. 7:9**

E. Testing is always based on resistance.

Jas. 1:12

Blessed is the man that endureth temptation: for when he is tried, he shall receive the crown of life, which the Lord hath promised to them that love him.

1. Your ability to resist the devil is proportionate to your submission to the Lord.

Jas. 4:7

Submit yourselves therefore to God. Resist the devil, and he will flee from you.

2. Without submitting to the Lord in the morning, there is no ability to resist the devil in the afternoon.

Ps. 63:1

O God, thou art my God; early will I seek thee . . .

F. Dreams and persecution.

1. Joseph identified with the dream God gave him.

Gen. 37:6

And he said unto them, Hear, I pray you, this dream which I have dreamed.

2. His brothers identified with the flesh — their personal desires.

Gen. 37:8

And his brethren said to him, Shalt thou indeed reign over us? or shalt thou indeed have dominion over us? and they hated him yet more for his dreams, and for his words.

3. Their fleshly orientation produced:

   a. Jealousy.

   Gen. 37:11

   And his brethren envied him;

   b. Persecution.

   Gen. 37:23,24

   . . . they stripped Joseph out of his coat, his coat of many colors that was on him; And they took him, and cast him into the pit . . .

4. They identified Joseph with their own selfish spirits, and attributed to him the motives of their own hearts.

Gen. 50:15

And when Joseph's brethren saw that their father was dead, they said, Joseph will peradventure hate us, and will certainly requite us all the evil which we did unto him.

Tit. 1:15

Unto the pure all things are pure: but unto them that are defiled and unbelieving is nothing pure; but even their mind and conscience is defiled.

G. Perseverence will always outlast persecution.

Jas. 1:4

But let patience have her perfect work, that ye may be perfect and entire, wanting nothing.

I Pet. 5:10

But the God of all grace, who hath called us unto his eternal glory by Christ Jesus, after that ye have suffered a while, make you perfect, stablish, strengthen, settle you.

Also **Phil. 2:8-11; Jas. 1:4; II Cor. 4:17; Rom. 8:18,37; I Pet. 1:6**

1. Perseverence - a prerequisite for a hero of faith.

Jas. 1:12

Blessed is the man that endureth temptation: for when he is tried, he shall receive the crown of life, which the Lord hath promised to them that love him.

Heb. 10:36

For ye have need of patience, that, after ye have done the will of God, ye might receive the promise.

Also **Heb. 12:1; Matt. 10:22**

a. Joseph's faith outlasted his life.

Heb. 11:22

By faith Joseph, when he died, made mention of the departing of the children of Israel; and gave commandment concerning his bones.

b. He made his children promise they would carry his bones to the Promised Land.

Gen. 50:25

And Joseph took an oath of the children of Israel, saying, God will surely visit you, and ye shall carry up my bones from hence.

Josh. 24:32

And the bones of Joseph, which the children of Israel brought up out of Egypt, buried they in Shechem, the parcel of ground which Jacob bought of the sons of Hamor . . .

Also **Exod. 13:19**

Chapter 1 (cont.)

2. Joseph knew —

a. What God authors He will finish.

Phil. 1:6

Being confident of this very thing, that he which hath begun a good work in you will perform it until the day of Jesus Christ.

Heb. 12:2

Looking unto Jesus the author and finisher of our faith . . .

b. What God promises He will fulfill.

Num. 23:19

God is not a man, that he should lie; neither the son of man, that he should repent: hath he said, and shall he not do it? Or hath he spoken, and shall he not make it good?

Also **Jude 24; Jas. 1:17**

c. What is committed to Him, He will keep.

II Tim. 1:12

. . . for I know whom I have believed, and am persuaded that he is able to keep that which I have committed unto him against that day.

Jude 24

Now unto him that is able to keep you from falling, and to present you faultless before the presence of his glory with exceeding joy.

Also **Titus. 1:2**

H. Joseph can be your role-model.

1. God wants you to be a hero of faith.

Heb. 11:6

But without faith it is impossible to please him: for he that cometh to God must believe that he is, and that he is a rewarder of them that diligently seek him.

Chapter 1 (cont.)

2. God-given dreams in God-favored men make a God-blest world.

Eph. 2:10

For We are his workmanship, created in Christ Jesus unto good works, which God hath before ordained that we should walk in them.

Deut. 8:18

But thou shalt remember the Lord thy God: for it is he that giveth thee power to get wealth, that he may establish his covenant which he sware unto thy fathers.

Also **Luke 11:9,10**

3. This is how God's Kingdom comes to earth through us.

Luke 11:2

. . . *Thy kingdom come, Thy will be done as in heaven, so in earth.*

Chapter 2 - MARCHING TO A DIFFERENT DRUMMER

A. Joseph was a spiritual achiever — an overcomer.

1. Mediocre men settle for good, which is the enemy of best.
2. God's transcendent glory filled Joseph's life.

Gen. 39:2,3

And the Lord was with Joseph, and he was a prosperous man . . . the Lord made all that he did to prosper in his hand.

a. This glory helped develop his potential.

Example: **Gen. 39:21,22**

But the Lord was with Joseph, and showed him mercy, and gave him favor in the sight of the keeper of the prison. And the keeper of the prison committed to Joseph's hand all the prisoners that were in the prison; and whatsoever they did there, he was the doer of it.

Also **Rom. 8:28**

b. God gives grace to sinners, and glory to saints.

Rom. 5:20

. . . But where sin abounded, grace did much more abound.

John 17:22

And the glory which thou gavest me I have given them;

Also **II Pet. 1:3; II Cor. 3:18**

B. Joseph possessed three qualities necessary to turn a God-given dream into reality: Favor, wisdom and courage.

1. Favor.

a. Favor with man:

Gen. 37:3

Now Israel loved Joseph more than all his children . . . and he made him a coat of many colors.

Also **Gen. 39:3-6**

b. Favor with God

See **Gen. 39:2;**

Gen. 41:39

And Pharaoh said unto Joseph, Forasmuch as God hath showed thee all this, there is none so discreet and wise as thou art:

i. God's favor is always bestowed as a gift.

Ps. 5:12

For thou, Lord, wilt bless the righteous; with favor wilt thou compass him as with a shield.

Ps. 89:17 (Living)

. . . Our power is based on your favor.

ii. It is called unmerited favor — or God's grace.

Eph. 2:8

For by grace are ye saved through faith; and that not of yourselves: it is the gift of God:

II Tim. 1:9

Who hath saved us, and called us with a holy calling, not according to our works, but according to his own purpose and grace.

iii. God gave Joseph authority and ability, He caused everything Joseph did to prosper, and Joseph rose to a position of leadership everywhere he went.

See **Gen. 39:3-6; 39:22,23; 40:4; 41:12,13; 41:39-42**

2. Wisdom

a. Wisdom is the principal thing.

Prov. 4:7

Wisdom is the principal thing; therefore get wisdom: and with all thy getting get understanding.

b. Wisdom provides for the totality of a man's life.

Prov. 3:16,17 (Living)

Wisdom gives: A long, good life, Riches, Honor, Pleasure, Peace

Also **Prov. 3:13-26; Prov. 8:14-21**

c. Wisdom must be sought after.

Prov. 8:17 (Living)

I (Wisdom) love all who love me. Those who search for me shall surely find me.

Also **Prov. 4:5; Prov. 2:1-7**

d. By devoting ourselves to Christ and all He has taught, we become men of wisdom.

Col. 2:3

In whom are hid all the treasures of wisdom and knowledge.

I Cor. 1:30

But of him are ye in Christ Jesus, who of God is made unto us wisdom, and righteousness, and sanctification and redemption.

Jas. 1:5

If any of you lack wisdom, let him ask of God, that giveth to all men liberally, and upbraideth not, and it shall be given him.

e. We must take time to meditate.

Josh. 1:8

This book of the law shall not depart out of thy mouth; but thou shalt meditate therein day and night, that thou mayest observe to do according to all that is written therein: for then thou shalt make thy way prosperous, and then thou shalt have good success.

Also **Ps. 1:2,3; Ps. 119:15**

i. Meditation is the matrix of creativity.

I Tim. 4:15

Meditate upon these things; give thyself wholly to them; that thy profiting may appear to all.

Ps. 1:2,3

But his delight is in the law of the Lord; and in his law doeth he meditate day and night. And he shall be like a tree planted by the rivers and water, that bringeth forth his fruit of his season; his leaf also shall not wither; and whatsoever he doeth shall prosper.

ii. We must discipline our minds to keep wild thoughts from intruding into our time with God.

II Cor. 10:5

Casting down imaginations, and every high thing that exalteth itself against the knowledge of God, and bringing into captivity every thought to the obedience of Christ.

Also **Exod. 19:12,13**

3. Courage

a. Courage is acting on a need greater than self.

Example: **Esth. 4:8,16**

Also he gave him the copy . . . of the decree that was given at Shushan to destroy them, to show it unto Esther, . . . and to charge her that she should go in unto the king, to make supplication unto him, and to make request before him for her people . . .
. . . And so will I go unto the king, which is not according to the law: and if I perish, I perish.

Also **Dan 3:16-18; I Sam. 17:32**

b. Why we need courage.

i. To face reality.

Ps. 51:6

Behold, thou desirest truth in the inward parts: and in the hidden part thou shalt make me to know wisdom.

ii. To make decisions.

Josh. 24:15

. . . choose you this day whom ye will serve; . . . but as for me and my house, we will serve the Lord.

Also **I Kings 18:21; Esth. 4:8,16**

Chapter 2 (cont.)

iii. To change.

Example: King Asa - **II Chron. 15:8**

And when Asa heard these words, and the prophecy of Oded the prophet, he took courage, and put away the abominable idols out of all the land of Judah and Benjamin, and out of the cities which he had taken from mount Ephraim, and renewed the altar of the Lord . . .

Also **Jonah 3:4-9; Gen. 12:1-4**

iv. To hold convictions.

Acts. 4:18-20

And they called them, and commanded them not to speak at all nor teach in the name of Jesus. But Peter and John answered and said unto them, Whether it be right in the sight of God to hearken unto you more than unto God, judge ye, for we cannot but speak the things which we have seen and heard.

Also **Phil. 1:27,28; Dan. 3:16-18; Dan. 6:10; Neh. 6:10,11**

v. To admit wrong or need.

Prov. 28:13

He that covereth his sins shall not prosper: but whoso confesseth and fosaketh them shall have mercy.

C. You will always live to the level of your faith.

1. Not everyone lives at the same level of faith.

Rom. 12:3,6
. . . according as God hath dealt to every man the measure of faith . . .
Having then gifts differing according to the grace that is given to us, whether prophecy, let us prophesy according to the proportion of faith;

2. A ministry grows to the level of its leader.

Matt. 10:24,25

The disciple is not above his master, nor the servant above his lord.
It is enough for the disciple that he be as his master, and the servant as his lord. . . .

3. As your faith level rises, your friendships change. This is the price of growth.

   II Pet. 1:1

   Simon Peter, a servant and an apostle of Jesus Christ, to them that have obtained like precious faith with us...

4. Retaining associations with those who will not grow can frustrate and discourage growth in our own lives.

   II Cor. 6:14

   Be ye not unequally yoked together with unbelievers:...

   Also **II Tim. 2:16**

5. We can be intimidated by other men's philosophies which are rationalizations to justify failures. When you accept such philosophies, you accept their failures.

   See **Ps. 1:1 ;Col.2:8**

   a. God wants us to grow from glory to glory so we can fulfill our dream.

      II Cor. 3:18

      But we all, with open face beholding as in a glass the glory of the Lord, are changed into the same image from glory to glory, even as by the Spirit of the Lord.

   b. Don't let anyone else's unbelief, rejection of truth, or refusal to grow, stop your dream.

      Example: **Num. 13:30** - Caleb

      And Caleb stilled the people before Moses and said, Let us go up at once, and possess it (the Land), for we are well able to overcome it. But the men that went up with him said, we be not able to go up against the people; for they are stronger than we.

      i. Grow with God.

         Acts 20:32

         And now, brethren, I commend you to God, and to the word of his grace, which is able to build you up, and to give you an inheritance among all them which are sanctified.

      ii. Grow in grace.

         II Pet. 3:18

         But grow in grace, and in the knowledge of our Lord and Savior Jesus Christ. To him be glory both now and for ever. Amen.

Chapter 2 (cont.)

iii. Grow in truth.

Prov. 23:23

Buy the truth, and sell it not; also wisdom, and instruction, and understanding.

Chapter 3 - YOUR LIFE HAS POTENTIAL

A. Everything in life holds potential.

1. Something is not created from nothing. It is made from things that are not seen.

   Heb. 11:3

   Through faith we understand that the worlds were framed by the word of God, so that things which are seen were not made of things which do appear.

2. Things that cannot be seen which are eternal are far more important than things that can be seen which are temporal.

   II Cor. 4:18

   While we look not at the things which are seen, but at the things which are not seen: for the things which are seen are temporal; but the things which are not seen are eternal.

3. Whether or not potential is developed depends on the invisible qualities we put into that potential: vision, faith, ingenuity, knowledge, talent and effort.

   Example: **Luke 9:12-17** - Jesus feeding the multitude.

B. Exchange is the process of life, and the process for the development of potential.

   Luke 19:12,13,15

   . . . A certain nobleman went into a far country . . . And he called his ten servants, and delivered them ten pounds, and said unto them, Occupy (trade with this) till I come . . . when he was returned . . . he commanded these servants to be called to him . . . that he might know how much every man had gained by trading.

1. This principle centers in the Cross of Christ.

2. Jesus came in His righteousness, became identified with our sins so that we, through repentance and faith, could become identified with His righteousness.

   II Cor. 5:21

   For he hath made him to be sin for us, who knew no sin; that we might be made the righteousness of God in him.

3. Calvary only holds potential for salvation, until you develop it by exchanging your sins for God's righteousness.

II Cor. 5:19,20; 6:1,2,

To wit, that God was in Christ, reconciling the world unto himself, not imputing their trespasses unto them; . . . we pray you, in Christ's stead, be ye reconciled to God . . .

C. Spiritual achievers (overcomers)

Rev. 3:21

To him that overcometh will I grant to sit with me in my throne, even as I also overcame, and am set down with my Father in his throne.

1. Spiritual achievers are doers of the Word.

Rev. 2:26

And he that overcometh, and keepeth my works unto the end, to him will I give power over the nations:

Also **Jas. 1:22-25; Matt. 7:21;**

2. They begin with what they have, while others moan because of what they don't have.

John 6:5-11

When Jesus then lifted up his eyes and saw a great company come unto him, he saith unto Philip, Whence shall we buy bread, that these may eat? . . .
Philip answered him, Two hundred pennyworth of bread is not sufficient for them . . .
And Jesus took the loaves; and when he had given thanks, he distributed to the disciples, and the disciples to them that were set down; and likewise of the fishes as much as they would.

D. Faith attracts the positive, fear attracts the negative.

1. Faith is believing what you cannot see will come to pass.

Heb. 11:1

Now faith is the substance of things hoped for, the evidence of things not seen.

2. Fear is believing that what you cannot see will come to pass.

Job. 3:25

For the thing which I greatly feared is come upon me, and that which I was afraid of is come unto me.

Chapter 3 (cont.)

E. Joseph's dream had potential.

1. It became a reality because he put faith in his dream.

Gen. 42:9

And Joseph remembered the dreams which he had dreamed of them . . .

Also **Gen. 45:7,8; Gen. 50:20**

2. His faith in God made it possible for him to put faith in his God-given dream.

Gen. 45:5

Now therefore be not grieved, nor angry with yourselves, that ye sold me hither: for God did send me before you to preserve life.

3. He knew without faith in his dream it would not become a reality.

Chapter 4 - CONVERT YOUR NEGATIVES INTO POSITIVES

A. God never ends anything on a negative.

1. Example: Joseph's life.

Gen. 50:20 (Living)

As far as I am concerned, God turned into good what you meant for evil, for he brought me to this high position I have today so that I could save the lives of many people.

2. When God created Adam, he was perfect in his humanity.

Gen. 1:27

So God created man in his own image, in the image of God created he him; . . .

3. When God completed His Creation, it was good, so He rested from His work.

see **Gen. 1:31, 2:2**

4. From then until now, peace has always been the umpire of doing the will of God.

Col. 3:15 Ampl.

And let the peace (soul harmony that comes) from the Christ rule (act as umpire continually) in your hearts — deciding and settling with finality all questions that arise in your minds . . .

B. The characteristics of the Kingdom emanate from the character of the King.

Prov. 29:2

When the righteous are in authority, the people rejoice: but when the wicked beareth rule, the people mourn.

1. All characteristics of God's Kingdom are positive.
   a. Light - **Rev. 21:23; Isa. 60:19; I Pet. 2:9; I John 1:5**
   b. Life - **John 11:25; John 17:2; John 20:31; John 10:10b**
   c. Love - **I John 4:8; Rom. 5:8; I John 3:1**
   d. Truth - **Deut. 32:4; Isa. 65:16; John 14:6**
   e. Obedience - **Dan. 7:27; Matt. 5:19b; Luke 11:2**

2. All characteristics of Satan's Kingdom are negative.
   a. Darkness - **Col. 1:13; Eph. 6:12**
   b. Death - **Rev. 20:14; John 10:10a**
   c. Lust - **John 8:44**
   d. Lying - **John 8:44**
   e. Disobedience - **Eph. 2:2**

C. Since the fall of Adam, conversion is necessary to human life.

1. We are negative by nature because we are conditioned to failure and subject to sin.

Rom. 5:18a, 19a

Therefore as by the offense of one, judgment came upon all men to condemnation . . .
For as by one man's disobedience many were made sinners . . .

Also **I Cor. 15:22**

2. We must be converted in all areas of our life: attitudes, habits, thought patterns, emotions, relationships, appetites, etc.

Rom. 12:2

And be not conformed to this world: but be ye transformed by the renewing of your mind, that ye may prove what is that good, and acceptable, and perfect, will of God.

Also **II Cor. 3:18**

D. Expectancy is the atmosphere for miracles.

Example: **Acts 3:5 -** The lame man at Gate Beautiful

And he gave heed unto them, expecting to receive something of them.

1. Positive words of faith create expectancy which prepares for the miraculous.

Example: **Acts 3:4**

And Peter, fastening his eyes upon him with John, said, Look on us.

2. Unbelief stifles the release of the miraculous.

Mark 6:5,6 - Jesus

And he could there do no mighty work, save that he laid his hands upon a few sick folk, and healed them.
And he marveled because of their unbelief . . .

E. Communication is the basis of life.

1. When communication stops, abnormality sets in.

John 15:6a

If a man abide not in me, he is cast forth as a branch, and is withered;

2. The ultimate end of abnormality is death.

   John 15:6b

   . . . and men gather them, and cast them into the fire, and they are burned.

3. Only reconciliation can bring renewed communication.

   See **II Cor. 5:20 - 6:2**

F. Repentance and reconciliation.

1. Repentance is the pivotal point between ruin and reconciliation.

   Acts 3:19

   Repent ye therefore, and be converted, that your sins may be blotted out, when the times of refreshing shall come from the presence of the Lord;

2. If you have lost communication with God through sin, repent and you will be reconciled to God, and restored to your proper place in the Kingdom.

   See **Luke 15:11-24** - Parable of the Prodigal

Chapter 5 - CHARACTER BUILDING BLOCKS

A. Character is always more important than talent.

Prov. 22:1

A good name is rather to be chosen than great riches, and loving favor rather than silver and gold.

Also **I Cor. 2:1-4**

1. Humanity tends to major on externals rather than the internal.

Matt. 23:25

Woe unto you, scribes and Pharisees, hypocrites! for ye make clean the outside of the cup and of the platter, but within they are full of extortion and excess.

John 7:24

Judge not according to the appearance, but judge righteous judgment.

2. The world puts a premium on talent, not character.

II Cor. 5:12

For we commend not ourselves again unto you, but give you occasion to glory on our behalf, that ye may have somewhat to answer them which glory in appearance, and not in heart.

3. The value of anything is internal rather than external.

Matt. 23:27,28

Woe unto you, scribes and Pharisees, hypocrites! for ye are like unto whited sepulchers, which indeed appear beautiful outward, but are within full of dead men's bones, and of all uncleanness.

B. Factors which build character.

1. A right relationship to God which enables one to receive revelation.

John 14:21,23

He that hath my commandments, and keepeth them, he it is that loveth me: and he that loveth me shall be loved of my Father, and I will love him, and will manifest myself to him.
. . . If a man love me, he will keep my words: and my Father will love him, and we will come unto him, and make out abode with him.

2. Crisis.

   a. God used crises to build Joseph's character.

   See **Gen. 50:20: Ps. 105:17-22**

b. Crisis is normal to life.

John 16:33

. . . In the world ye shall have tribulation: but be of good cheer; I have overcome the world.

c. It takes us from the transient to the permanent.

I Pet. 1:6,7

. . . though for a season, if need be, ye are in heaviness through manifold temptations: That the trial of your faith, being much more precious than of gold that perisheth, though it be tried with fire, might be found unto praise and honor and glory at the appearing of Jesus Christ:

3. Sorrow.

a. Sorrow is one of life's greatest teachers.

Eccl. 7:3

Sorrow is better than laughter: for by sadness of the countenance the heart is made better.

Ps. 119:71

It is good for me that I have been afflicted; that I might learn thy statutes.

b. Joseph's submission was not to the circumstances, but to the God of transcendent glory who is able to take each sorrow and ultimately make it work for good.

Rom. 8:28

And we know that all things work together for good to them that love God, to them who are the called according to his purpose.

Also **Phil. 1:12,13,19**

c. God is able to take things that are not and make them into things that are for His glory.

Rom. 4:17

. . . even God, who quickeneth the dead, and calleth those things which be not as though they were.

d. God can take your life just as it is, and make something special of it, and bring glory to His name.

Example: **II Sam. 7:8** - David

Now therefore so shalt thou say unto my servant David, Thus saith the Lord of hosts, I took thee from the sheepcote, from following the sheep, to be ruler over my people, over Israel:
And I was with thee whithersoever thou wentest, and have cut off all thine enemies out of thy sight, and have made thee a great name, like unto the name of the great men that are in the earth.

4. A genuine desire for God.

Ps. 63:1,8

O God, thou art my God; early will I seek thee: my soul thirsteth for thee, my flesh longeth for thee in a dry and thirsty land, where no water is;
My soul followeth hard after thee: . . .

Heb. 11:6

. . . he is a rewarder of them that diligently seek him.

Also **Ps. 42:1,2,; Ps. 84:2; Jer. 29:13.**

a. Anger towards sin and a desire to reprove it.

Ps. 101:3

I will set no wicked thing before mine eyes; I hate the work of them that turn aside; it shall not cleave to me.

b. Willingness to face persecution rather than capitulate to sin.

I Pet. 4:1

Forasmuch then as Christ hath suffered for us in the flesh, arm yourselves likewise with the same mind: for he that hath suffered in the flesh hath ceased from sin;

Also **Heb. 12:3,4**

C. God requires faithfulness — He will provide you with ability.

II Tim. 2:2

And the things that thou hast heard of me among many witnesses, the same commit thou to faithful men, who shall be able to teach others also.

Also **I Cor. 4:2; I Tim. 1:12**

1. God never gives authority without accountability.

    Luke 12:48

    . . . For unto whomsoever much is given, of him shall be much required:

    Rom. 14:12

    So then, every one of us shall give account of himself to God.

    Also **Matt. 18:23; Luke 19:15** (Authority/Accountability)

2. Christlikeness is the ultimate good that God's transcendent glory works to produce.

    Rom. 8:29

    For whom he did foreknow, he also did predestinate to be conformed to the image of his Son, that he might be the firstborn among many brethren.

    Also **II Cor. 3:18**

3. Your value to God is in the Christlikeness of your character.

    II Tim. 2:20,21

    But in a great house there are not only vessels of gold and of silver, but also of wood and of earth; some to honor, and some to dishonor.
    If a man therefore purge himself from these, he shall be a vessel unto honor, sanctified, and meet for the master's use, and prepared unto every good work.

Chapter 6 - IMAGE, IMAGE ON MY MIND

A. Images have a powerful influence on our lives.

Prov. 23:7

For as he thinketh in his heart, so is he . . .

Also **Ps. 115:4-8; Tit. 1:15** (Living)

1. One of the most important things you can do in life is create an image.

   Ps. 115:4-8

   . . . They that make them (images) are like unto them; so is every one that trusteth in them.

2. The next most powerful thing you can do is destroy it.

   Num. 33:52

   Then ye shall drive out all the inhabitants of the land from before you, and destroy all their pictures . . .

3. Joseph's God-given dream established an image in his mind of who he was and who he was to become.

   Gen. 37:5-11

   And Joseph dreamed a dream, and he told it to his brethren: and they hated him yet the more . . .
   For behold, we were binding sheaves in the field, and, lo, my sheaf arose, and also stood upright; and, behold, your sheaves stood round about, and made obeisance to my sheaf . . .
   And he dreamed yet another dream, and told it his brethren, and said, Behold, I have dreamed a dream more; and, behold, the sun and the moon and the eleven stars made obeisance to me.

4. Our experiences in our early years create images and have great influence upon us as adults.

   Example: **II Tim. 1:5; II Tim. 3:15**

   When I call to remembrance the unfeigned faith that is in thee, which dwelt first in thy grandmother Lois, and thy mother Eunice; and I am persuaded that in thee also . . .
   And that from a child thou hast known the holy scriptures, which are able to make thee wise unto salvation through faith which is in Christ Jesus.

5. When we teach children to discern right from wrong it is vital we do it correctly.

Prov. 22:6

Train up a child in the way he should go: and when he is old, he will not depart from it.

B. Our images must be renewed.

Eph. 4:22,23

That ye put off . . . the old man, which is corrupt according to the deceitful lusts; And be renewed in the spirit of your mind:

1. When you change an image you change behavior, and changing behavior changes feelings.

II Cor. 5:17

Therefore if any man be in Christ, he is a new creature: old things are passed away; behold, all things are become new.

2. Those who succeed in life have healthy self-images.

Example: **I Sam. 17:32** - David

C. Your image of God is the most influential image.

1. God wants us to know him personally, intimately.

Jas. 4:8

Draw nigh to God, and he will draw nigh to you . . .

2. We have a problem if our image of God is given to us through sermons, denominational traditions and doctrines of men.

Col. 2:8

Beware lest any man spoil you through philosophy and vain deceit, after the tradition of men, after the rudiments of the world, and not after Christ.

I Cor. 1:5

That your faith should not stand in the wisdom of men, but in the power of God.

D. All our lives we must battle the imposition of other's images of what we should be, and what the Church should be.

Example: **I Sam. 17:28,29**

. . . Eliab's anger was kindled against David, and he said, Why camest thou down hither? and with whom hast thou left those few sheep . . . I know thy pride and the naughtiness of thine heart; for thou art come down that thou mightest see the battle.

Chapter 6 (cont.)

1. We can be seriously restricted by other's images of ourselves.

   Example: **Gen. 37:19,20**

   And they said one to another, Behold this dreamer cometh.

   Come now therefore, and let us slay him, and cast him into some pit, . . . and we shall see what will become of his dreams.

2. We must daily seek God's Word, so our images are from God and not from man.

   Rom. 12:2

   And be not conformed to this world: but be ye transformed by the renewing of your mind, that ye may prove what is that good, and acceptable, and perfect, will of God.

   II Cor. 3:18

   But we all, with open face beholding as in a glass the glory of the Lord, are changed into the same image from glory to glory . . .

3. It is Jesus Christ who died for our sins, shed His blood, and was raised from the dead to redeem us unto God. He has the right of ownership over us, and His Church.

   I Cor. 6:20

   For ye are bought with a price: therefore glorify God in your body, and in your spirit, which are God's.

   Also **I Pet. 1:18-21**

4. What should really count in your life is not what you or others think, but what God thinks.

   John 5:44

   How can ye believe, which receive honor one of another, and seek not the honor that cometh from God only?

Chapter 7 - THE WAY UP IS DOWN

A. Leadership is service.

Matt. 20:25-28

. . . whosoever will be great among you, let him be your minister;
And whosoever will be chief among you, let him be your servant.

1. We are only qualified to lead to the degree we are willing to serve.

Luke 22:25-27

. . . but he that is greatest among you, let him be as the younger; and he that is chief, as he that doth serve.
For whether is greater, he that sitteth at meat, or he that serveth? is not he that sitteth at meat? but I am among you as he that serveth.

Also **John 13:13-16**

2. The more we serve the greater we become.

Matt. 23:11

But he that is greatest among you shall be your servant.

3. How we care for others is the measure of our own greatness.

Luke 9:47,48

. . . Whosoever shall receive this child in my name receiveth me: and whosoever shall receive me receiveth him that sent me: for he that is least among you all, the same shall be great.

Also **Matt. 24:45-47**

4. A father's greatness with his family is based on his care for them.

Example: **Gen. 18:19** - Abraham

For I know him, that he will command his children and his household after him, and they shall keep the way of the Lord . . .

Also **Eph. 6:4**

B. Serving is not servitude, it is a voluntary subscription of love.

Phil. 2:5-9

Let this mind be in you, which was also in Christ Jesus:
Who, being in the form of God, thought it not robbery to be equal with God:
But made himself of no reputation, and took upon him the form of a servant, and was made in the likeness of men
And being found in the fashion as a man, he humbled himself . . .

1. Love is a characteristic of God's Kingdom. Love desires to give.

I John 4:9,10

In this was manifested the love of God toward us, because that God sent his only begotten Son into the world, that we might live through him.
Herein is love, not that we loved God, but that he loved us, and sent his Son to be the propitiation for our sins.

2. Lust is a characteristic of Satan's Kingdom; lust desires to get.

John 8:44

Ye are of your father the devil, and the lusts of your father ye will do. . . .

Prov. 27:20

Hell and destruction are never full . . .

3. Those in leadership have the potential for good or harm.

Prov. 29:2

When the righteous are in authority, the people rejoice: but when the wicked beareth rule, the people mourn.

Also **I Chron. 28:8,9; Eccl. 10:5**

C. There are four levels we can live on in life.

1. Assumption - life's lowest level of knowledge.

Matt. 13:19

When any one heareth the word of the kingdom, and understandeth it not, then cometh the wicked one, and catcheth away that which was sown in his heart.

Isa. 5:13

Therefore have my people gone into captivity, because they have no knowledge: . . .

2. Knowledge - knowing the facts but not living them.

Ezek. 33:30-32

. . . And they come unto thee as the people cometh, and they sit before thee as my people, and they hear thy words, but they will not do them: . . .
And, lo, thou art unto them as a very lovely song of one that hath a pleasant voice, . . . for they hear thy words, but they do them not.

Also **Jas. 1:22-24**

3. Ability - able to act on knowledge, but we don't make it a part of our life.

Matt. 7:26

And every one that heareth these sayings of mine, and doeth them not, shall be likened unto a foolish man, which built his house upon the sand:

4. Practice - The highest learning level. Our knowledge is part of our lifestyle. Leadership is lived at this level.

Matt. 7:24

Therefore whosoever heareth these sayings of mine, and doeth them, I will liken him unto a wise man, which built his house upon a rock:

Also **Jas. 1:25**

D. Limitations of leadership.

1. The knowledge of his own mind.

Ps. 119:99

I have more understanding than all my teachers: for thy testimonies are my meditation.

II Tim. 2:15

Study to show thyself approved unto God, a workman that needeth not to be ashamed, rightly dividing the word of truth.

2. The worth of his own character.

II Tim. 2:21

If a man therefore purge himself from these, he shall be a vessel unto honor, sanctified, and meet for the master's use, and prepared unto every good work.

Also **Luke 16:10-12; I Cor. 4:2**

3. The principles upon which he is building his own life.

Prov. 4:5-8

Get wisdom, get understanding: forget it not; neither decline from the words of my mouth.
Forsake her not, and she shall preserve thee: love her, and she shall keep thee. Wisdom is the principal thing; therefore get wisdom: and with all thy getting get understanding.

Also **Ps. 119:133**

4. Leadership requires knowledge, character and principles.

Ezra 7:10

For Ezra had prepared his heart to seek the law of the Lord, and to do it, and to teach in Israel statutes and judgments.

E. There can be no effective public denunciation unless there is first a private renunciation.

Example: **Luke 4:12-15** - Jesus

And when the devil had ended all the temptation he departed from him for a season.
And Jesus returned in the power of the Spirit into Galilee: and there went out a fame of him through all the region round about.

1. The leader must first practice what he wants others to do before they will follow him.

I Tim. 4:12

Let no man despise thy youth; ***but be thou an example*** *of the believers, in word, in conversation (manner of life), in charity, in spirit, in faith, in purity.*

I Pet. 5:3

Neither as being lords over God's heritage, ***but being examples*** *to the flock.*

2. Taking up, not giving up - is the issue of leadership.

Matt. 16:24,25

. . . If any man will come after me, let him deny himself, and take up his cross, and follow me.
For whosoever will save his life shall lose it: and whosoever will lose his life for my sake will find it.

Also **Luke 9:23; Matt. 10:38,39**

3. When you accept God's requirements you come into agreement with Him. The place of agreement is the place of power.

   Matt. 18:19

   Again I say unto you, that if two of you shall agree on earth as touching any thing that they shall ask, it shall be done for them of my Father which is in heaven.

4. Joseph was a leader with a servant's heart. His entire life was one of serving others.

   See **Gen. 39:3-5,22; Gen. 40:4**

Chapter 8 - CONFESSION IS GOOD FOR YOU

A. You are committed to what you confess.

1. Confession to confirm our faith.

Rom. 10:8,9

. . . The word is nigh thee, even in thy mouth, and in thy heart: that is, the word of faith, which we preach; That if thou shalt confess with thy mouth the Lord Jesus, and shalt believe in thine heart that God hath raised him from the dead, thou shalt be saved.

2. Confession of appreciation.

a. Gratitude and appreciation are forms of praise.

Col. 3:15

Let the peace of God rule in your hearts . . . ***and be ye thankful.***

b. Praise brings God into your circumstances and relationships.

Ps. 22:3

But thou art holy, O thou that inhabitest the praises of Israel.

c. Failing to express appreciation brings the sin of omission.

Jas. 4:17

Therefore to him that knoweth to do good, and doeth it not, to him it is sin.

3. Confession must be balanced.

a. Confession of sin must be balanced by faith.

Acts 20:21

Testifying both to the Jews, and also to the Greeks, repentance toward God, and faith toward our Lord Jesus Christ.

Heb. 6:1

. . . not laying again the foundation of repentance from dead works, and faith toward God.

i. Confess out your sin.

I John 1:9

If we confess our sins, he is faithful and just to forgive us our sins, and to cleanse us from all unrighteousness.

ii. Confess in your righteousness.

Ps. 107:2

Let the redeemed of the Lord say so, whom he hath redeemed from the hand of the enemy.

b. What you believe is what you confess.

Luke 6:45

A good man out of the good treasure of his heart bringeth forth that which is good; and an evil man out of the evil treasure of his heart bringeth forth that which is evil: for out of the abundance of the heart his mouth speaketh.

Also **Matt. 12:34,35**

B. Life is composed of your choices and constructed by your words.

Prov. 21:23

Whoso keepeth his mouth and his tongue, keepeth his soul from troubles.

Also **Prov. 15:4**

1. Words are the expression of our life.

Luke 6:45

. . . out of the abundance of the heart his mouth speaketh.

2. We are the sum total of all the words we have ever spoken, or those spoken to us which we have received into our lives.

Prov. 18:21

Death and life are in the power of the tongue: and they that love it shall eat the fruit thereof.

Also **Prov. 23:7**

3. God upholds all things by the word of His power.

Heb. 1:3

Who being the brightness of his glory, and the express image of his person, and upholding all things by the word of his power, . . .

4. Every word spoken has power to create in the positive or in the negative.

Mark 11:23

. . . he shall have whatsoever he saith.

Prov. 6:2

thou art snared with the words of thy mouth, thou art taken with the words of thy mouth.

Also **Matt. 12:37**

C. God-given dreams, and the confessing of them, is the process God uses to accomplish his purposes.

Chapter 9 - IT'S IN YOUR MOUTH

A. Hypocrisy - a "mask wearer."

Luke 12:1

. . . Beware ye of the leaven of the Pharisees, which is hypocrisy.

1. Applies to a person who says one thing with his mouth, and then lives in another manner entirely.

Matt. 23:2,3

. . . The scribes and the Pharisees sit in Moses' seat: . . .
. . . do not ye after their works: for they say, and do not.

Also **Jer. 7:9,10**

2. Applies to a person who believes one thing in his heart, but says another with his mouth.

Matt. 15:7,8

Ye hypocrites, well did Isaiah prophesy of you, saying, This people draweth nigh unto me with their mouth, and honoreth me with their lips; but their heart is far from me.

3. Moral cowardice: one who does not want to confess Christ publicly, because he does not want to commit himself to living the life.

John 12:42,43

Nevertheless among the chief rulers also many believed on him; but because of the Pharisees they did not confess him, lest they should be put out of the synagogue:
For they loved the praise of men more than the praise of God.

B. Confession has potential for good or harm.

Matt. 12:37

For by thy words thou shalt be justified, and by thy words thou shalt be condemned.

1. Example: the rash vow.

Eccl. 5:4-6

When thou vowest a vow unto God, defer not to pay it; for he hath no pleasure in fools; pay that which thou hast vowed.
Better is it that thou shouldest not vow, than that thou shouldest vow and not pay. Suffer not thy mouth to cause thy flesh to sin . . .

Example: Jephthah's vow - **Judges 11:30,31,36**

2. Confession of our worthiness in Christ.

   See **II Cor. 5:21**

   a. Based on grace, not works.

      Eph. 2:8

      For by grace are ye saved through faith; and that not of yourselves: it is the gift of God:

      Also **Tit. 3:5**

   b. Founded on trust in God to meet your needs.

      Phil. 4:19

      But my God shall supply all your need according to his riches in glory by Christ Jesus.

      Ps. 23:1

      The Lord is my shepherd; I shall not want.

   c. Enables us to receive great things from God.

      Eph. 3:20

      Now unto him that is able to do exceeding abundantly above all that we ask or think, according to the power that worketh in us.

C. Receiving is as important as believing.

1. If after believing, you cannot receive, you nullify your believing.

   Mark 11:24

   . . . What things soever ye desire, when ye pray, believe that ye receive them, and ye shall have them.

2. Joseph didn't create the dream. He simply received it when God gave it.

3. Believe God for great things, then receive those things from God.

   Luke 12:32

   . . . it is your Father's good pleasure to give you the kingdom.

Chapter 10 - MASTER YOUR PASSION

A. Mastering your passion.'

Gal. 5:16

This I say then, Walk in the Spirit, and ye shall not fulfill the lust of the flesh.

1. Everyone has a master passion.

Gal. 5:17

For the flesh lusteth against the Spirit, and the Spirit against the flesh: and these are contrary the one to the other: so that ye cannot do the things that ye would.

Examples:

a. sex.

II Tim. 2:22

Flee also youthful lusts: but follow righteousness . . .

b. power.

Luke 4:5-8

(vs. 6) And the devil said unto him, All this power will I give thee, and the glory of them: . . .

c. pleasure.

II Tim. 3:4

. . . lovers of pleasure more than lovers of God.

2. Your spur-of-the-moment decisions are rooted and grounded in your character.

Prov. 4:23

Keep thy heart with all diligence; for out of it are the issues of life.

3. The true measure of your character is expressed not by what you do in public, but what you think about when you are alone - your meditations, fantasies, dreams.

Ezek. 8:12

Then said he unto me, Son of man, hast thou seen what the ancients of the house of Israel do in the dark, every man in the chambers of his imagination? for they say, The Lord seeth us not; . . .

Phil. 4:8

Finally, brethren, whatsoever things are true, whatsoever things are honest, whatsoever things are pure, whatsoever things are of good report; if there be any virtue, and if there be any praise, think on these things.

4. Impure actions are the consequence of impure thoughts, meditations, desires, appetites residing in a man's spirit.

   Matt. 12:35

   A good man out of the good treasure of the heart bringeth forth good things: and an evil man out of the evil treasure bringeth forth evil things.

   Jas. 1:14,15

   But every man is tempted, when he is drawn away of his own lust, and enticed.
   Then when lust hath conceived, it bringeth forth sin: and sin, when it is finished, bringeth forth death.

5. Generally, the *sin of omission* - not praying and meditating on God's Word - prohibits the character of Christlikeness from coming forth in times of temptation.

   Jas. 1:21

   Wherefore lay apart all filthiness and superfluity of naughtiness, and receive with meekness the engrafted word, which is able to save your souls.

6. The test of our lives is what we do when we're alone with our master passion.

   Example: **Gen. 39:11,12**

   And it came to pass about this time, that Joseph went into the house to do his business; and there was none of the men of the house within.
   And she caught him by his garment, saying lie with me: and he left his garment in her hand, and fled, and got him out.

B. The Spirit of the Spoiler.

1. Satan is a spoiler.

   John 8:44

   Ye are of your father the devil, and the lusts of your father ye will do. He was a murderer from the beginning, . . .

   a. He spoils everything he touches.

      John 10:10a

      The thief cometh not, but for to steal, and to kill, and to destroy: . . .

b. He wants to possess you.

Luke 22:31

And the Lord said, Simon, Simon, behold, Satan hath desired to have you, that he may sift you as wheat: . . .

c. He wants to take the place of God.

Isa. 14:12-15

How are thou fallen from heaven, O Lucifer, son of the morning! . . .
For thou hast said in thine heart, I will ascend into heaven, I will exalt my throne above the stars of God . . .
I will ascend above the heights of the clouds; I will be like the most High.

2. His first weapon is temptation.

Mark 1:12,13

And immediately the Spirit driveth him into the wilderness.
And he was there in the wilderness forty days, tempted of Satan; . . .

a. Temptation is generally persistent. You may have to battle the same thing over and over again.

Eph. 6:12

For we wrestle not against flesh and blood, but against principalities, against powers, against the rulers of the darkness of this world, against spiritual wickedness in high places.

Also **James 4:7; I Pet. 5:8,9**

b. It is not a sin to be tempted.

Example: **Luke 4:1,2,** - Jesus

And Jesus being full of the Holy Ghost returned from Jordan, and was led by the Spirit into the wilderness, Being forty days tempted of the devil . . .

c. Sin is only conceived when we succumb to temptation by letting our hearts be drawn away with it.

Jas. 1:14,15

But every man is tempted, when he is drawn away of his own lust, and enticed.
Then when lust hath conceived, it bringeth forth sin: and sin, when it is finished, bringeth forth death.

d. The true test is what we do with the temptation and its author.

Prov. 1:10

My son, if sinners entice thee, consent thou not.

Jas. 4:7

Submit yourselves therefore to God.
Resist the devil, and he will flee from you.

Also **Rom. 6:12,13; Matt. 26:41**

3. Satan's second weapon is accusation.

Rev. 12:10

. . . for the accuser of our brethren is cast down, which accused them before our God day and night.

a. Satan's accusations are often based on half truths.

Example: **Zech. 3:1,3**

And he showed me Joshua the high priest standing before the angel of the Lord, and Satan standing at his right hand to resist him . . .
Now Joshua was clothed with filthy garments, . . .

b. When he accuses you, you must counter those accusations with the truth.

Zech. 3:2

And the Lord said unto Satan, The Lord rebuke thee, O Satan; even the Lord that hath chosen Jerusalem rebuke thee: is not this (Joshua) a brand plucked out of the fire?

c. Jesus Christ is the justifier of the brethren.

I Cor. 6:11

And such were some of you: but ye are washed, but ye are sanctified, but ye are justified in the name of the Lord Jesus, and by the Spirit of our God.

Also **Rom. 3:26; Rom. 5:1**

C. Truth vs. the lie.

1. It is easier to believe a lie than the truth, because man is negative by nature.

John 3:19

And this is the condemnation, that light is come into the world, and men loved darkness rather than light . . .

II Thes. 2:10

. . . because they received not the love of the truth, . . .

2. Truth will always triumph; it may be defeated for a time, but it will never die.

    Prov. 12:19

    The lip of truth shall be established for ever: but a lying tongue is but for a moment.

    Also **Ps. 100:5**

3. The truth was Joseph's vindication. God knew the truth and vindicated him.

    See **Gen. 41:39-44**

D. The criteria of holiness is the honor of God.

1. Joseph was not concerned about himself, but about the honor of God.

    Gen. 39:9

    . . . how then can I do this great wickedness, and sin against God?

2. Courage is sometimes expressed in a decision to flee.

    Gen. 39:12

    And she caught him by his garment, saying, Lie with me: and he left his garment in her hand, and fled, and got him out.

    Also **II Tim. 2:22; I Cor. 6:18**

Chapter 11 - IS GOD MAD AT YOU?

A. Wrong believing about God.

1. Some believe God is against them because He convicts them of sin.

Heb. 12:5

. . . My son, despise not thou the chastening of the Lord, nor faint when thou art rebuked of him:

a. Conviction of sin is an evidence of God's love.

Heb. 12:6

. . . for whom the Lord loveth he chasteneth, and scourgeth every son whom he receiveth.

b. He wants us to forsake sin so He can bring us a greater revelation of Himself, and become more intimate with us.

I Cor. 11:32

When we are judged, we are chastened of the Lord, that we should not be condemned with the world.

Also **Ps. 94:12,13**

2. Many feel God is their adversary based on guilt and condemnation.

a. Actually Satan is the accuser.

See **Rev. 12:10**

b. Satan accuses God to man and man to God to put distance between them.

See **Zech. 3:1-3; Job. 1:78**

3. Some feel God is mad at them based on circumstantial evidence in their lives.

Judges 6:13 - Example

And Gideon said unto him, Oh my Lord, if the Lord be with us, why then is all this befallen us? . . .

4. Wrong believing about God will keep you from having an intimate relationship with Him.

Matt. 11:6

Blessed is he, whosoever shall not be offended in me.

B. The three levels of knowledge of God.

1. God is for me.

Ps. 56:9

When I cry unto thee, then shall mine enemies turn back: this I know; for God is for me.

Also **Rom. 8:31**

2. God is with me.

Ps. 23:4

Yea, though I walk through the valley of the shadow of death, I will fear no evil: for thou art with me; . . .

Also **Matt. 1:23**

3. God is in me.

Col. 1:27

. . . which is Christ in you, the hope of glory:

Phil. 2:13

For it is God which worketh in you both to will and to do of his good pleasure.

a. God indwells me by His Holy Spirit.

I Cor. 6:19

What? know ye not that your body is the temple of the Holy Ghost which is in you, which ye have of God, and ye are not your own?

b. God is at work at all times to produce our highest good, His perfect will.

Rom. 8:28

And we know that all things work together for good to them that love God, to them who are called according to his purpose.

Also **Phil. 2:12,13; Ps. 139**

C. What you believe about God has the greatest potential for good or harm in your life.

Rom. 1:16

For I am not ashamed of the gospel of Christ: for it is the power of God unto salvation to every one that believeth; . . .

Rom. 1:21

Because that, when they knew God, they glorified him not as God, neither were thankful; but became vain in their imaginations, and their foolish heart was darkened.

1. What you believe can attract or repel.

See **Job. 3:25; Mark 11:23**

2. What you believe determines relationships.

   a. What you believe about God will determine your relationship with Him.

      Heb. 11:6

      . . . for he that cometh to God must believe that he is, and that he is a rewarder of them that diligently seek him.

   b. What you believe about yourself will determine your relationships with others.

      Prov. 23:7

      . . . for as he thinketh in his heart, so is he: . . .

3. Joseph believed God was a good God. God loved him, and God was working on his behalf.

   See **Gen. 45:5; Gen. 50:20; Ps. 105:17-22**

Chapter 12 - WHEN THE INNOCENT SUFFER FOR THE GUILTY

A. The innocent suffering for the guilty.

Gen. 40:15 Living - Joseph

For I was kidnapped from my homeland among the Hebrews, and now this - here I am in jail when I did nothing to deserve it.

1. It is one thing to suffer as guilty when you are; it's another to suffer when you are innocent.

I Pet. 2:20

For what glory is it, if, when ye be buffeted for your faults, ye shall take it patiently? but if, when ye do well, and suffer for it, ye take it patiently, this is acceptable with God.

Also **I Pet. 3:14,15; Matt. 5:11,12**

B. What to do when forced to suffer for the guilt of others.

1. Realize the situation has potential for good as well as harm.

See **Rom. 8:28**

2. Realize Jesus Christ bore all the hurt, bitterness, shame and resentment on the Cross.

Isa. 53:4,5

But he was wounded for our transgressions, he was bruised for our iniquities: the chastisement of our peace was upon him; and with his stripes we are healed.

Also **Heb. 12:2; I Pet. 2:21,22**

3. Recognize how much God has forgiven you.

Ps. 103:11,12

For as the heaven is high above the earth, so great is his mercy toward them that fear him.
As far as the east is from the west, so far hath he removed our transgressions from us.

Jer. 31:34

. . . I will forgive their iniquity, and I will remember their sin no more.

4. Forgive those who have harmed you, so you can release their sins out of your life.

Mark 11:25

And when ye stand praying, forgive, if ye have aught against any: that your Father also which is in heaven may forgive you your trespasses.

Also **Matt. 5:23,24; John 20:22,23**

Chapter 12 (cont.)

5. Submit the circumstances to God instead of rebelling against them.

I Pet. 2:23 - Jesus

Who, when he was reviled, reviled not again; when he suffered, he threatened not; but committed himself to him that judgeth righteously.

I Pet. 5:6,7

Humble yourselves therefore under the mighty hand of God, that he may exalt you in due time:
Casting all your care upon him; for he careth for you.

Chapter 13 - SET A PRIORITY OR TWO

A. The pressure principle.

1. Pressure always magnifies.

   Example: **Luke 22:42-44**

   Saying, Father, if thou be willing, remove this cup from me: nevertheless not my will, but thine be done.
   . . . And being in an agony he prayed more earnestly: and his sweat was as great drops of blood falling down to the ground.

2. The difference in men who succeed and men who fail is in their ability to handle pressure.

   Example: **Luke 22:54-57** - Peter's denial.

   . . . But a certain maid beheld him as he sat by the fire, and earnestly looked upon him, and said, This man was also with him.
   And he denied him, saying, Woman, I know him not.

   Example: **I Sam. 30:6** - David

   And David was greatly distressed; for the people spake of stoning him, because the soul of all the people was grieved, every man for his sons and for his daughters: but David encouraged himself in the Lord his God.

3. Jesus faced the ultimate pressure and triumphantly overcame it. Therefore whoever believes in Him and receives His Spirit can live in the same way.

   Heb. 12:2,3

   Looking unto Jesus the author and finisher of our faith; who for the joy that was set before him endured the cross, despising the shame, and is set down at the right hand of the throne of God.
   For consider him that endured such contradiction of sinners against himself, lest ye be wearied and faint in your minds.

   Also **Phil. 2:8,9**

B. Priorities.

1. Men who become heroes must also have a value system in which their priorities are set aright.

   Matt. 6:33

   But seek ye first the kingdom of God, and his righteousness; and all these things shall be added unto you.

   Also **Dan. 6:7-10**

Chapter 13 (cont.)

2. Some things in life are more important than life itself.

   Matt. 20:28

   Even as the Son of man came . . . to give his life a ransom for many.

   Also **Matt. 10:39**

3. This principle has the potential for good or harm.

   Example:

   a. John the Baptist - faced execution rather than compromise truth.

      See **Matt. 14:3-11**

   b. Stephen - stoned for his stand for righteousness.

      See **Acts 7:54-60**

   c. Jesus Christ - gave His life for our salvation.

      See **John 10:17,18**

   d. Esau - sold his birthright for a mess of pottage.

      Gen. 25:29-34

   e. Eli - lost his life and ministry because he indulged his sons at the expense of the Word of God.

      See **I Sam. 2 and 3**

Chapter 14 - ARE YOU READY TO PROSPER?

A. Money.

1. What you believe about money will attract or repel it.

   Prov. 11:24,28

   There is that scattereth, and yet increaseth; and there is that withholdeth more than is meet, but it tendeth to poverty . . .

2. Money is amoral. We give it morality or immorality.

   Luke 16:9

   And I say unto you, Make to yourselves friends of the mammon of unrighteousness; that, when ye fail, they may receive you into everlasting habitations.

   I Tim. 6:17

   Charge them that are rich in this world, that they be not high-minded, nor trust in uncertain riches, but in the living God, who giveth us richly all things to enjoy.

3. Money has the potential for blessing or cursing. Money is a means, not an end.

   Prov. 22:9

   He that hath a bountiful eye shall be blessed; for he giveth of his bread to the poor.

   Matt. 6:24

   No man can serve two masters: for either he will hate the one, and love the other; or else he will hold to the one, and despise the other. Ye cannot serve God and mammon.

4. The *lust* of money is the root of all evil.

   I Tim. 6:10

   For the (covetous, avaricious) love of money is the root of all evil: which while some coveted after, they have erred from the faith, and pierced themselves through with many sorrows.

B. Tithing.

1. Money is not all there is to tithing. Tithing is not all there is to stewardship.

Example: **II Cor. 8:1,3,5**

Moreover, brethren, we do you to wit of the grace of God bestowed on the churches of Macedonia; . . .
For to their power, . . . yea, and beyond their power they were willing of themselves; . . .
And this they did, not as we hoped, but first gave their own selves to the Lord, and unto us by the will of God.

2. Tithing time, talent and treasury.

I Cor. 6:19,20

. . . ye are not your own? For ye are bought with a price: therefore glorify God in your body, and in your spirit, which are God's.

3. Three reasons why men won't tithe money:

a. Unbelief.

Mal. 3:10

Bring ye all the tithes into the storehouse, . . . and prove me now . . . if I will not open you the windows of heaven, and pour you out a blessing, . . .

b. Fear.

Mal. 3:11

And I will rebuke the devourer for your sakes . . .

c. Covetousness.

Mal. 3:8

Will a man rob God? Yet ye have robbed me . . . In tithes and offerings.

4. Giving is a release to the spirit.

See **Isa. 58:6-8**

5. Giving is an expression of love.

See **II Cor. 8:1-4**

6. You know the depth of love by the degree of giving.

John 3:16

For God so loved the world, that he gave his only begotten Son, that whosoever believeth in him should not perish, but have eternal life.

John 15:13

Greater love hath no man than this, that a man lay down his life for his friends.

7. Offerings are not for the health of the preacher, but for the health of the congregation.

   Prov. 3:9,10

   Honor the Lord with thy substance, and with the firstfruits of all thine increase:
   so shall thy barns be filled with plenty, and thy presses shall burst out with new wine.

8. God's purpose in prospering His people is not for them to gain, but so more can be given to the work of the Lord.

   II Cor. 9:8,10,11 Living

   . . . Yes, God will give you much so that you can give away much, and when we take your gifts to those who need them they will break out into thanksgiving and praise to God for your help.

C. You cannot compensate by sacrifice what you lose through disobedience.

   I Sam. 15:22

   . . . Behold, to obey is better than sacrifice, and to hearken than the fat of rams.

1. If we love Jesus we'll obey Him.

   John 14:15

   If you love me, keep my commandments.

2. Obedience is the evidence of love.

   John 14:21a,

   He that hath my commandments, and keepeth them, he it is that loveth me:

3. Manifestation is based on obedience.

   John 15:21b,23

   . . . and he that loveth me shall be loved of my Father, and I will love him, and will manifest myself to him . . .
   . . . If a man love me, he will keep my words: and my Father will love him, and we will come unto him, and make our abode with him.

4. Prayer will not bring God's financial blessings if you are disobeying God by not tithing.

   Ps. 66:18

   If I regard iniquity in my heart, the Lord will not hear me:

Chapter 14 (cont.)

5. The offering and the altar are synonymous.
   a. You give your life to Jesus at the altar once.

      See **Matt. 10:39**

   b. You continue to give your life to God by placing your life in the offering plate.

      See **II Cor. 9:12,13** Living

      . . . for this (is) proof that your deeds are as good as your doctrine.

6. The issue isn't being rich or poor, but being obedient. Money only holds potential.

Chapter 15 - GUILT? WHO NEEDS IT?

A. Guilt.

1. The results of sin: Guilt, Fear and Hiding.

   Gen. 3:9,10

   And the Lord God called unto Adam, and said unto him, Where art thou?
   *And he said, I heard thy voice in the garden, **and I was afraid**, because **I was naked**; and **I hid myself.***

2. You cannot get the guilt out of your life until you ask God to forgive you.

   Example **Ps. 32:3-5** Living

   *There was a time when I wouldn't admit what a sinner I was. But my dishonesty made me miserable and filled my days with frustration . . . until I finally admitted all my sins to you and stopped trying to hide them. I said to myself, "I will confess them to the Lord." And you forgave me! **All my guilt is gone.***

   a. When we confess our sins, God forgives us, and no longer holds them against us.

   I John 1:9

   If we confess our sins, he is faithful and just to forgive us our sins, and to cleanse us from all unrighteousness.

   b. By the help of God, through the presence of His Holy Spirit, you can forgive others as God forgives you.

   John 20:22,23

   . . . Receive ye the Holy Ghost:
   Whosoever sins ye remit, they are remitted unto them; and whosoever sins ye retain, they are retained.

3. Because they had never asked for and received forgiveness, Joseph's brothers could not release their guilt.

   Gen. 50:15

   When Joseph's brethren saw that their father was dead, they said, Joseph will peradventure hate us, and will certainly requite us all the evil which we did unto him.

4. Guilt kills relationships.

B. Forgiveness

1. When Jesus Christ forgives our sins, they are severed from us.

Ps. 103:12

As far as the east is from the west, so far hath he removed our transgressions from us.

Isa. 43:25

I, even I, am he that blotteth out thy transgressions for mine own sake, and will not remember thy sins.

2. If God forgives us and we do not forgive ourselves, then we make ourselves greater than God.

Rom. 8:33,34

Who shall lay anything to the charge of God's elect? It is God that justifieth.
Who is he that condemneth? It is Christ that died, yea rather, that is risen again, who is even at the right hand of God, who also maketh intercession for us.

3. There is joy in releasing our guilt to Jesus.

Ps. 51:7,12

Purge me with hyssop, and I shall be clean: wash me, and I shall be whiter than snow . . .
Restore unto me the joy of thy salvation; and uphold me with thy free Spirit.

a. We are free from guilt.

Heb. 10:22

Let us draw near with a true heart in full assurance of faith, having our hearts sprinkled from an evil conscience . . .

b. Free to love.

I Cor. 13:5 (Ampl.)

. . . Love (God's love in us) does not insist on its own rights or its own way, for it is not self-seeking; it is not touchy or fretful or resentful; it takes no account of the evil done to it - pays no attention to a suffered wrong.

c. Free to worship and serve God.

Heb. 9:14

How much more shall the blood of Christ, who through the eternal Spirit offered himself without spot to God, purge your conscience from dead works to serve the living God?

Chapter 16 - THE PRICE OF PEACE

A. Being nice is not always being loving.

1. Conviction of sin and chastening are manifestations of love.

   See **Prov. 3:11,12**

   a. Sin left in our lives prevents God's intimacy with us.

      Jas. 4:7,8

      Draw nigh to God, and he will draw nigh to you. Cleanse your hands, ye sinners; and purify your hearts, ye double-minded.

   b. Without sorrow for sin there cannot be repentance.

      II Cor. 7:9,10

      Now I rejoice, not that ye were made sorry, but that ye sorrowed to repentance:
      for ye were made sorry after a godly manner, . . . For godly sorrow worketh repentance to salvation not to be repented of: . . .

   c. Without repentance there cannot be reconciliation and fellowship with God.

      Isa. 55:7

      Let the wicked forsake his way, and the unrighteous man his thoughts: and let him return unto the Lord, and he will have mercy upon him; and to our God, for he will abundantly pardon.

2. Peace and passivity are not the same.

   John 14:27

   Peace I leave with you, my peace I give unto you: not as the world giveth, give I unto you. . . .

3. We are to love our enemies, but not capitulate to them.

   Rom. 12:19-21

   . . . Be not overcome of evil, but overcome evil with good.

4. Peace at any price is devilish, not divine.

   Matt. 10:34

   Think not that I am come to send peace on earth: I came not to send peace, but a sword.

5. Truth must always be spoken in love.

   Eph. 4:15

   But speaking the truth in love, may grow up into him in all things, . . .

B. Identification with Christ.

1. We lose our life by finding it in identification with Jesus Christ.

Luke 9:24,25

. . . For whosoever will save his life shall lose it: but whosoever will lose his life for my sake, the same shall save it.

2. If we don't make the decision to identify with Christ we cannot receive from God, and our God-consciousness is non-existent.

See **II Tim. 2:11,12; Matt. 12:30; Matt. 10:32,33**

C. Joseph's identification with God.

1. Joseph knew who he was in his identification with God.

See **Gen. 45:5**

2. When everything was going wrong for him, he knew who he was and he knew God had spoken to him.

See **Gen. 50:20**

3. Joseph's faith outlasted his life.

Heb. 11:22

By faith Joseph, when he died, made mention of the departing of the children of Israel; and gave commandment concerning his bones.

"If your principles for lifetime goals are not in line with God and His Word, it's time to rechart your direction."

EDWIN LOUIS COLE —

Internationally acclaimed speaker, television personality, bestselling author and motivational lecturer, known for his practical application of wisdom from kingdom principles.

Ed Cole has been called to speak with a prophetic voice to men, challenging them to fulfill their potential for true manhood, which is Christlikeness. He now travels extensively, exhorting young men to realize their dreams by disciplining themselves to God's favor, wisdom and courage.

To receive Dr. Cole's publication,
COURAGE, write:

EDWIN LOUIS COLE MINISTRIES
P. O. Box 610588
Dallas, Texas 75261

EDWIN LOUIS COLE
AUDIO TEACHING TAPES

AGREEMENT: THE PLACE OF POWER **$20.00**
(4 tapes)
To release power in your life, you must be in agreement with yourself, with God, with the others involved — the principle is from Matthew 18 and affects every area of life.

RELEASED **$10.00**
(2 tapes)
How do you spell "Release"? Learn to forgive so you can be free from guilt, fear, and strongholds of sin in your life.

STRAIGHT TALK: X-RATED **$10.00**
(2 tapes)
Sex sins — get them out of your life and be free to live with peace instead of guilt. Tapes to listen to whenever you are tempted.

MAXIMIZED MANHOOD SEMINAR **$20.00**
(4 tapes)
Taped live during a TV Satellite Seminar, this is the message from the book, "Maximized Manhood," plus plus plus. Study these!

THE POTENTIAL PRINCIPLE SEMINAR **$20.00**
(4 tapes)
Live from a TV Seminar, this is the series about your future. You are taking care of yourself today — these will prepare you for success tomorrow.

A NEW AWAKENING **$20.00**
(4 tapes)
Experience the praise, teaching, and worship from the first National Christian Men's Event — join the 7,800 attendees of one of the largest men-only events in the history of the United States.

LEADERSHIP **$30.00**
(6 tapes)
The complete teaching from breath mints to Biblical exegesis. Start right, stay right with your church, Bible study group, or children's class. THIS IS A *MUST* FOR LEADERS!

COVENANT FULFILLMENT **$10.00**
(2 tapes)

Deep, penetrating teaching on Matthew 5:7 that emphasizes our worth through Christ, Who is worthy. (A-110)

FOR WOMEN ONLY **$10.00**
(2 tapes)

A provocative series that will help women understand themselves and become the godly women the Lord has called them to be. (A-111)

FOR PARENTS ONLY **$10.00**
(2 tapes)

Draws lessons from the life of Eli, concerning the responsibility God places on the man in the home, and warns of the tragic consequences for the whole family when the father neglects his God-given authority. (A-112)

A NEW AWAKENING **$20.00**
(4 tapes)

Relive the praise, teaching and worship of the 1984 National Christian Men's Event, held in Houston, Texas. One of the largest "men only" gatherings ever held in the United States. (A-113)

POTENTIAL PRINCIPLE SEMINAR **$20.00**
(4 tapes)

Teaching on the plan God has for your success, based on the life of Joseph. Taped during a national satellite broadcast to over 800 churches. (A-114)

Available at your local bookstore.

Books By Edwin Louis Cole

Maximized Manhood

Maximized Manhood Study Guide

The Potential Principle

The Potential Principle
Scripture Reference Guide

COURAGE
A Book For Champions

Available at your local bookstore.

A Division of Harrison House, Inc.
P. O. Box 35035
Tulsa, OK 74153